SILK PAINTING

Books should be returned or renewed by the
last date stamped above

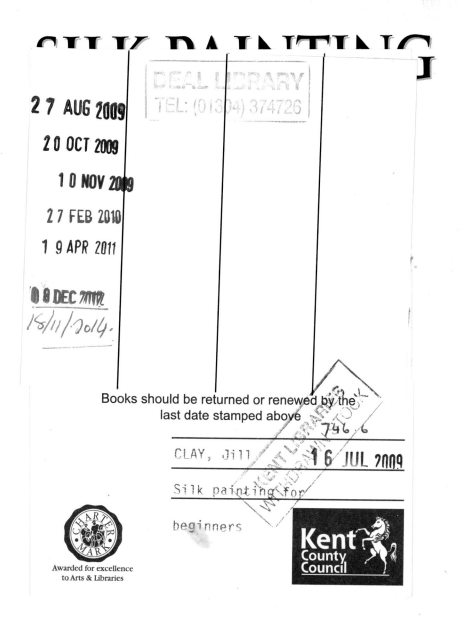

Awarded for excellence
to Arts & Libraries

Kent
County
Council

SILK PAINTING
for beginners

JILL CLAY

GUILD OF MASTER CRAFTSMAN PUBLICATIONS LTD

First published 2002 by
Guild of Master Craftsman Publications Ltd
166 High Street, Lewes
East Sussex, BN7 1XU

ISBN 1 86108 266 5
A catalogue record of this book is available from the British Library

Designed by Fran Rawlinson
Cover design by Fran Rawlinson
Typeface: Adobe Garamond

Origination and printing by Grafiche Torriani, Milan, Italy

I have all my students from the past 10 years to thank for this book. Without them as my willing guinea pigs, I could not have written it. In particular I would like to thank my students from the last two years: each chapter was sneakily tested out on them. Thanks. You know who you are!

Contents

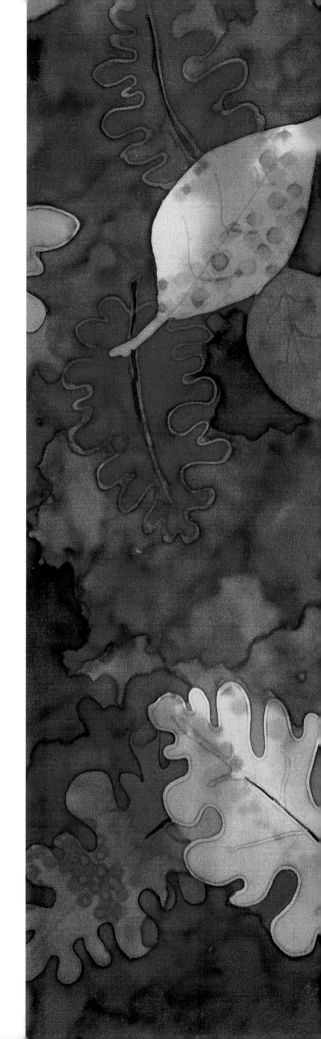

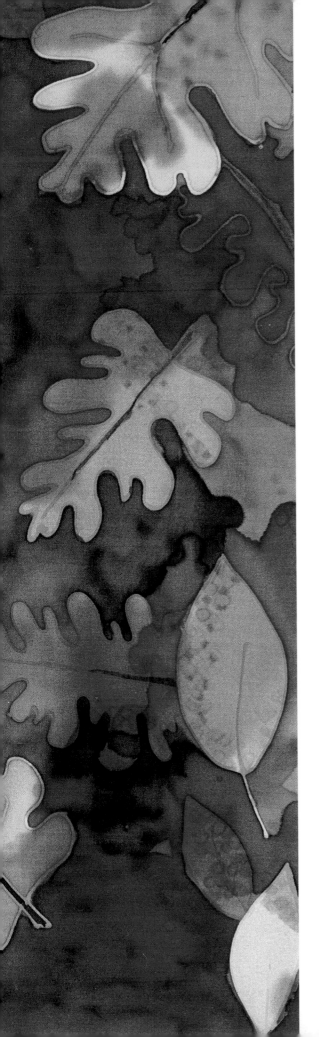

Creating patterns and textures

Fixing your dyes

A polarizer was used to reduce the surfa... clarity of the water graphically into the picture, ... almost as clearly below the water as you can above it.) However, th... some detail in the reflection of the mountain. In such circumstance... fast rule; at the time the decision can only be made by viewing t... rotating filter and choosing between none, half or a fully polari... the loss of some detail in the reflection is an acceptable pric... in the foreground.

Still water is often calmest very early in the morning, ...

Tachi...

Introduction

There are some odd words in the world of silk painting – gutta, pongee, habotai – but these will all soon become very familiar. My hope is to teach you the basics of this lovely art and encourage you to develop your own style. Artistic ability isn't necessary – if you can hold a paintbrush, and enjoy spending time on a relaxing task, this is the hobby for you. Always remember that there are very few mistakes that can't be reworked, and very few serious mistakes to be made. If you do make one, at the very least you will have learnt an important lesson, and you can apply this to future projects.

I'll take you through step by step and show you just how easy, and how satisfying, it is to produce pieces of work to be proud of.

'What's that then?'

Of course, you'll have to practise the techniques, but that's where the fun really starts. Silk painting is a great hobby. It's easy to get started and has only one hazard – you get hooked very quickly! One of the most exciting aspects is that you never know exactly how a piece will turn out.

Silk paints are available in stunning and vibrant colours, and I'll show you how to create beautiful textures with them. I have found there is a great fear of using steam-fix dyes; I hope to dispel the myth that they are hard to use and highlight the immeasurable difference between steam-fix and iron-fix dyes.

For all the work in this book I have used Arty's one dyes, but any steam-fix dye can be used. Arty's one are my personal favourite as I know they will produce all the effects I require. You should find no problem getting supplies through mail-order outlets, though if you ask your local art store they may be willing to stock some of the basic items for you; although silk painting is hardly a new idea, shops seem to be slow in stocking what is needed. Just keep asking and, with luck, you'll get them to see it your way.

Finally, painting should be relaxing, so don an old shirt, put on some music, and relax. I love the week-long courses I run where I get to see the progression from timid painters, using a tiny frame, to happy painters producing silk by the metre. I hope you get the same pleasure they do.

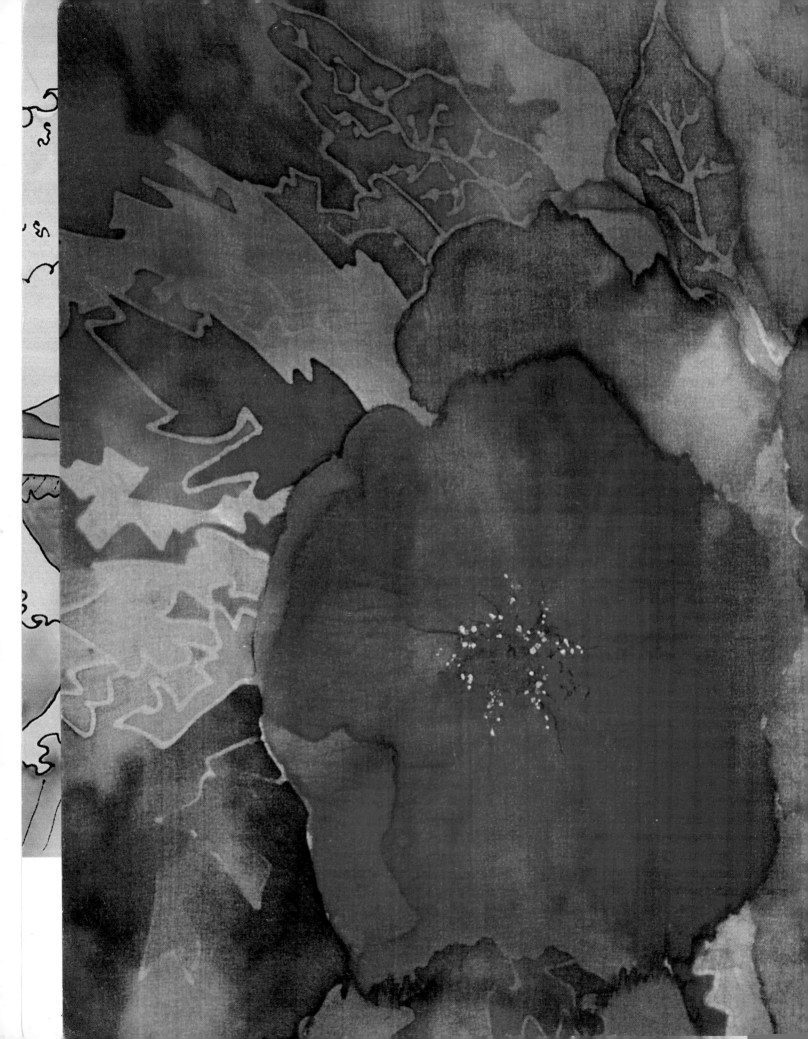

GETTING
EQUIPPED

Tools and equipment

Before you start your silk painting, you will need to have a few basic tools and pieces of equipment to hand. The most expensive items are not always the best; some you can even make yourself.

Working with frames

⚬ Frames should sit at least ½in (13mm) above the work surface so that the silk doesn't sag down and touch it as it gets wet. This would restrict the flow of dye and, of course, colour your worktop.

⚬ Cover your handmade frames with shiny brown parcel tape. This will enable you to wash down the frame after every painting.

Imagine that you have just finished a scarf with a black border and then start on a pretty pink scarf; if you haven't washed the frame, the dye left on it will transfer onto your new scarf as soon as it gets wet.

⚬ When making frames to fit a particular project, remember that pre-hemmed items can vary in size by as much as 2in (5cm).

BRUSHES

Many types of brush – from watercolour to Chinese – can be used for silk painting. As long as the brush has a reasonably thick base (so that it can hold plenty of colour) and a fine point (to enable detailed work) it will be suitable. Most of my favourites were very cheap. Use old brushes if you are applying gutta as an alternative to fabric paint, clean them immediately after use, and never let them go hard. There may be chemicals in the gutta that could damage the brush, and if it dries hard you will have to rub the bristles to relax the gutta, a process to which your brush won't take kindly. I would strongly recommend using your best brushes only for paint and dye. Foam brushes are useful but they do tend to soak up vast amounts of dye without later releasing it! For this reason they are best used for applying water.

MAINTENANCE
Clean all your brushes thoroughly after use by swirling them on a bar of soap and then rinsing several times. You can buy special brush soap, but if you rinse your brushes thoroughly after use, this isn't necessary. All you need to hold your water is an old jar. If you want to be extra careful use two jars, one for washing and one for rinsing. Stroke the bristles back into shape and leave to dry.

You need a tapered brush for silk painting

My students will vouch for the fact that my pet hate is brushes left in water. Even if left for just a short time, irreparable damage can be done. The bristles bend and there is nothing you can do to straighten them out. Always rinse out your brushes, leave them to dry, and lay them flat when they are not in use.

Try to keep a thin and a thick brush aside for both yellow and black as, even with careful cleaning, these dyes have a tendency to sit in the base of the brush and muddy other colours.

PINS

There are various types of pin available. As with most silk painting equipment you must try as many types as possible and experiment until you find which ones you prefer.

It is not a good idea to use ordinary drawing pins as they will break the delicate fibres of the silk and leave holes. A better option is pushpins; these have a very fine point that will not split the fibres. The most popular pins are the three-pronged ASSA pins which give a more secure hold. They also have a central hole which is extremely useful for adding dye to the hems on ready-made items; transfer the dye from your brush to the fabric through this hole. These pins do have a tendency to lose prongs as you're removing them from the frame, but you can continue to use them even when they have lost two. Do not run your fingers around the edge of the frame as it is very easy to cut them on the ends left from broken prongs. Remove any such ends with a pair of tweezers.

Stenter pins are another option, though they are a good deal more expensive than other pins. They have a plastic base with three, needle-sharp prongs that grip the silk leaving only the tiniest of holes. They are attached to the frame with an elastic band. I have found that elastic hairbands

ASSA pins have a reliable grip

GATHERING
MATERIALS

Silk

Silk is an amazing fabric. It will keep you warm in winter and cool in summer and, as a bonus, most silks are fully washable and resistant to mildew and moths. There is a huge range of silks on the market, from chiffon and crêpe de Chine to cord.

In order to select the right silk for the job, it is important that you understand the good and bad points of each type and the effect they have on dyes. Pongee 5 is perfect for beginners as it is reasonably cheap and very easy to get hold of. On the whole, fabrics with a fine weave accept gutta better, but heavier fabrics – habotai 12 and upward – are perfect for cards and pictures as the finished work is easier to cut and mount. As heavier fabrics have more body and substance, they tend to hold their shape once cut where lighter fabrics tend to be floppy.

Your fabric must be 100% silk or a mixture of silk and wool. Unfortunately, fabrics are not always labelled correctly; if you are unsure about the make-up of your silk, test it to be sure. This is an easy process, but for safety reasons, it should be done outside. Light a candle or a long match and hold the fabric over it, preferably at the end of a long pair of tongs. Pure silk will not burn well and will stop burning when it is removed from the flame. It will emit a smell similar to that of burning wool or feathers and leave a black residue, which should turn to powder when rubbed between your fingers. Any fabric with wool content will be quite thick – thicker even than heavyweight pure silk – and if the fabric contains man-made fibres it will burn to a ball or lump.

CUTTING TO SIZE

Don't cut your silk before seeing how to make the best use of it. Try out various ways of placing your frame on the silk to find which arrangement wastes the least fabric. You only need sufficient silk to allow it to be pinned securely. If you leave silk hanging over the edges of your frame it is not only wasteful, if it flaps up over your work it could smudge your gutta or dye.

Tear your silk rather than cutting the whole way through. Because silk is a soft and slick fabric, it tends to slip through the scissors and not cut a straight line. However, silk will tear in perfectly straight lines and the faster you tear the better. Cut a nick into your fabric, about 1in (2.5cm) long, hold the tips of the silk very

securely and tear quickly. Try to stop just before the end and snip the last few threads with scissors or they will pucker up and need straightening out. In lighter-weight fabrics, this straightening can weaken the fibres and cause them to break at the edges; the heavier the fabric, the easier it is to straighten them out without damage.

PINNING ONTO A FRAME

There are many ways of pinning silk onto your frame. If you are using Stenter pins or a plastic frame, you will find full instructions enclosed. I prefer the following method, but as I always say, you must experiment to find what suits you best. The important thing is that the silk be tight. If it is not tight, the dyes will not spread properly and if it is too tight, you will create grooves in which the dye will pool and form dark lines. Getting this right is something that will come with practice.

1 Square your silk up on the frame and stick a pin at each corner.

2 Working across the top of your frame, and without pulling the silk, stick one pin in every few inches (7–8cm), though if you feel happier using more pins, that's fine. What is important is that you don't pull the silk up at this stage or it will distort the shape.

3 Move to the opposite side and insert additional pins along it as well. This time, pull the silk down gently with one hand and stick a pin in with the other, trying to get it opposite a pin at the top of the frame.

4 Repeat this process for the remaining sides. This will result in a perfectly tight piece of silk.

PREVIOUS PAGE *Silk is available in a variety of finishes*
RIGHT *The shimmering colours of a dyed silk scarf*
FAR RIGHT *(from the top) Velvet, twill, crêpe de Chine*

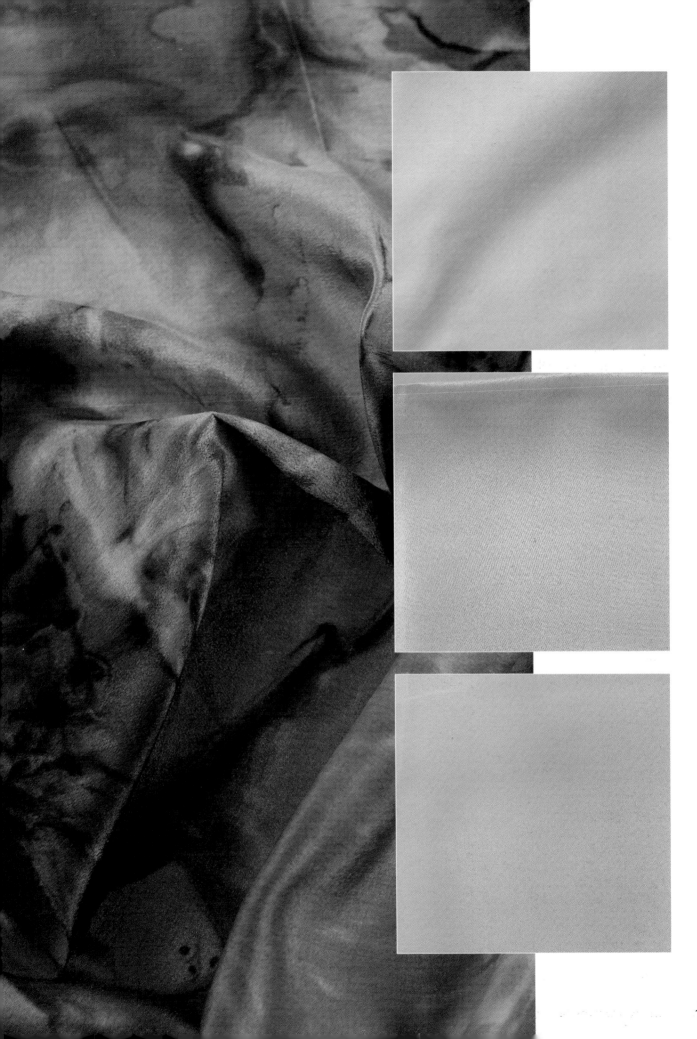

Silks and their uses

Chiffon 3.5/ Mousselline	Thin, diaphanous. Loose weave, therefore the colour will not spread as far. Works best when layered or folded	Light scarves, overblouses and window dressings
Pongee 5	The most useful silk for beginners. Thin, even weave. Becomes softer and more lustrous after steaming	Beginners' practice silk, light scarves, kites
Habotai 8	Heavier than pongee, more fibres. A great, all-round silk	Pictures, lampshades, cards and wall hangings
Jaquard	Elaborate silk with patterns woven into it to add depth and dimension	Clothing and cushions
Dupion	Dense fibres with irregular slubs	Wedding dresses, formal wear
Twill	Silk with diagonal weave	Scarves, cummerbunds and pictures
Crêpe de Chine	Classic drapery silk with a high lustre and open weave. Slightly stretchy. Hangs beautifully	All garments, accessories and wall hangings
Taffeta	Closely woven, lightweight silk with subtle sheen. Luxury alternative to habotai 8	Dresses, wedding dresses
Tussah	Made from wild moths whose diet is oak leaves. Colours range from cream to sand	Suits, jackets, pillows, upholstery and other interior décor
Raw silk/noil	Woven natural colour with uneven slabs. Soft and wrinkle resistant. Lightweight but strong. Uneven texture. Stiff in handling	Suits, jackets, trousers. Eveningwear and home furnishings

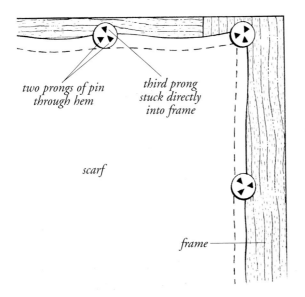

two prongs of pin through hem

third prong stuck directly into frame

scarf

frame

PINNING SCARVES TO FRAMES

Scarves should be pinned onto a frame with three-pronged pins. Insert two prongs through the hem and into the frame and the third prong just into the frame, as shown above. Pushing pins into the body of the scarf results in holes that can, over time, become much larger and spoil the design.

TAPING ONTO A FRAME

Silk can also be fixed to the frame with masking tape. The same rules apply as for pinning; tape one side first, then the opposite, and repeat on the final two sides. If you are desperate to paint and haven't got a frame, an old biscuit tin and a strong elastic band will do the trick.

WASHING AND PRESSING

Contrary to popular belief, silk benefits from regular washing as this restores its sheen. It is best handwashed, using a gentle handwash liquid. Washing by hand for a few minutes is a much gentler process than an hour in a washing machine. I use shampoo; after all, hair is a protein like silk. I also condition my silk with hair conditioner, though ordinary fabric softener will suffice. Always read your washing liquid bottle – some are not suitable for use on silk. If your silk has been steamed correctly, you can wash it in a washing machine without worrying about any dye loss.

Allow your silk to dry naturally until it is just damp and then iron it, with your iron on a wool setting. Don't iron any seams while they are still wet as they will become shiny. If possible, iron up to seams but not over them.

LEFT *Pinning a ready-hemmed scarf*
BELOW *Satin 11*
BOTTOM *Jaquard 16, spots*

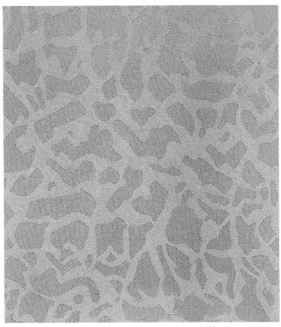

Dyes

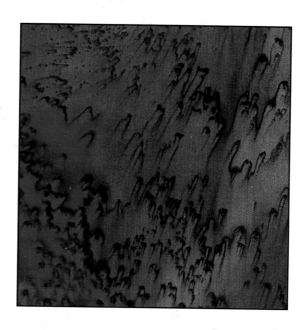

Which dye to use is a matter of personal choice – the most expensive is not necessarily the best. The two main types of dye for silk painting are steam-fix and iron-fix dyes.

Steam-fix dyes produce wonderfully lustrous colours

In order to make an appropriate selection, you need to know the good and bad points of each (see the Table on p 33). If you can, try every type of dye to find which you prefer, don't take other painters' word on the best type to use. Steam-fix dyes will work beautifully with all the techniques described in this book. (For fixing instructions see Fixing your dyes, p 118.)

STEAM-FIX DYES

Steam-fix dyes are transparent dyes that penetrate the fabric's fibres completely. The smallest amount will go an amazingly long way. You can add up to 20% water to most steam-fix dyes and still achieve the same brilliance of colour. However, there are some dyes that will separate into their individual components if you add water. Until you are familiar with all the different brands, it is a good idea to test for water tolerance.

TESTING FOR WATER TOLERANCE

1 Pin a piece of silk onto your frame and, using a pencil, draw on a grid of squares, 5 × 5.

2 Gutta the lines and leave to dry.

3 Pour about 10ml (⅓ US fl oz) of pure dye into your palette and paint the top left square.

4 Add four drops of water to the pure dye, mix thoroughly, then paint the next square.

5 Continue adding four more drops of water, mixing thoroughly and painting until each square has been filled. This will give you an idea of how far you can dilute your dyes to achieve various shades.

PREVIOUS PAGE '*Peacock*'

IRON-FIX DYES

Iron-fix dyes are opaque and very easy to use. Because they are paint rather than dye, they are thicker than steam-fix dyes and tend not to spread as far. While they don't work with many of the techniques described here, they do work brilliantly with salt and saline solutions. They can all be thinned down with water.

POURING DYES

Dye bottles come in many shapes and forms. Some have wide tops, others have integral pipettes. If your bottles don't have their own pipettes, use a plastic one. This will allow you to dispense small amounts of dye as required. Use a white ice-cube tray as a palette. These are great: they can hold up to 16 colours at a time, and have enough depth to hold larger amounts of dye, and the colours appear clear and true.

LEFTOVER DYES

You should never be in the situation where have to throw away steam-fix dyes. Even when you have added water to the colours in your palette, you can store leftover dyes for later use.

One way of doing this is to cover your palette with clingfilm or pop it carefully into a plastic bag, but remember that the colours will become

BELOW *White ice-cube trays make excellent palettes*
BOTTOM *Colour distillation*

stronger and more concentrated as the dyes dry out, so they might not remain the exact colours that you were using. When you next come to paint, water down the dyes and use as usual.

Another option is to store the dyes in wash bottles. Use baby-food jars, or better still, empty glass dye bottles with built-in droppers. You don't need dozens of wash bottles, with one for each colour; four would be sufficient, giving you one for each of the most common secondary and tertiary colours – orange, green, purple and brown. It is easy to transfer the dyes from palette to bottle if you suck them up with a pipette or dropper. Add anything that is basically red or a tone or shade of red to the orange bottle, anything that is green to the green bottle, and anything purple to the purple bottle; place any colour that you are unsure about in the brown bottle. You will be amazed at how much dye you end up with, dye that might otherwise have been washed down the sink. The major frustration is that you produce fantastic colours that you can never mix again. Use these dyes for ordinary painting, for painting backgrounds and for dip-dyeing.

Applying dyes

⚜ Rinse your brushes before you start painting, and before each new colour, to check that they are clean and free of dye.

⚜ To keep colours bright you must dry your brush thoroughly before dipping it into the dye.

⚜ To dilute dyes you must use pure or filtered water, diluent or alcohol, and always follow the manufacturer's instructions for both mixing and fixing.

⚜ The depth of colour of any dye increases after fixing. With practice you will become used to these changes in colour and paint your pictures accordingly.

⚜ Always try to dry your brushes to a point: this will make your painting much more accurate than a brush that is splayed out.

⚜ Make sure you have enough dye in your palette before you start to paint. This is safer even if you are using a colour straight from the tube. If you have to leave an area unfinished and then go back to it to add more paint, the first thing you'll get is a watermark. If you are using a colour you have mixed yourself, it is virtually impossible to mix the exact shade again.

⚜ Fill your brush right up to the bristles, then wipe it off on the side of the palette: trying to work with only a small amount of dye on your brush will actually make it harder (because you need to keep refilling it, it can lead to uneven colour and marks) but a dripping brush is one step away from disaster.

⚜ Don't have a cup of coffee next to your water pot: you can bet the cup is where you will dip your brush.

⚜ Never wash your brush and take it dripping across the top of your picture; keep your water and tissues for drying the brush on the same side as your painting hand.

⚜ Try to stay well away from the gutta lines. As gutta lines are not high barriers, it is quite easy for paint to flow over them. Apply the dye towards the centre of the area and allow it to spread to the line. If it doesn't reach the line, keep feeding colour into the dye that is already there until it does.

CHARACTERISTICS OF DYES

STEAM-FIX	IRON-FIX
Can easily be thickened	Have their own thickener to stop excess spreading
They give a beautiful smooth background when mixed with diluent	Almost impossible to achieve an even background on large pieces of work
Retain the softness of the silk after steaming	Silk can loose its lustre and softness after painting with some brands
Colours equally vibrant on both sides when used on light- and medium-weight fabrics	Reverse side is not usually as vibrant as top side
As there is no white steam-fix dye, must be diluted to achieve pastel shades	Have white as part of the colour range so pastels are easy to mix
Are fully mixable	Are fully mixable
Dry evenly	Tend to dry with slight patches
Can be diluted by 20% with no change in depth of colour	Can be diluted with water
Can be revitalized when dried out by adding water or diluent	Will go hard when dry and cannot be revitalized
Become even more vibrant when steamed	Steaming has no effect on colour
Easy to use, but require longer fixing process than iron-fix dyes	Easy and quick to use
Can only be used on silk	Certain brands can be used on silk, cotton, wool, linen and even some synthetics
Can be dry-cleaned	Can be dry-cleaned
Some are fade-resistant and machine washable after fixing	Some are fade-resistant and machine washable after fixing
Must be fixed with steam	Some brands can be fixed using a hairdryer

Gutta resist

Gutta Serti (gutta) is the drawing medium used in silk painting. It is used to keep colours separate and to outline designs. Guttas harden once they have soaked into the silk, thus forming a barrier that stops one colour from leaking into another.

There are two main types of gutta: water-based and spirit-based. I always recommend using water-based guttas as they have no odour and are easier to wash off your equipment. However, both can be used successfully with iron-fix and steam-fix dyes. Some types of gutta work better than others; experiment until you find one with a consistency that will allow it to flow yet still form a good resist line. In warm weather, keep your gutta in the fridge: if it gets too warm, it won't hold its line. Gutta is available as a transparent resist and in many colours, including black and metallic; it is now even possible to colour your own. Applying gutta is the most important stage of the silk painting process so don't hurry, you'll regret it: dye will squeeze through even the smallest gap in a gutta 'wall'.

COLOURING GUTTAS

Leave a little steam-fix dye in your palette overnight. The next day the dye will have become concentrated and very strong. Add just enough water to make it fluid again, then add this to clear gutta. In this way, you can produce many shades

PREVIOUS PAGE *'How many?'*
BELOW *Black and transparent guttas*

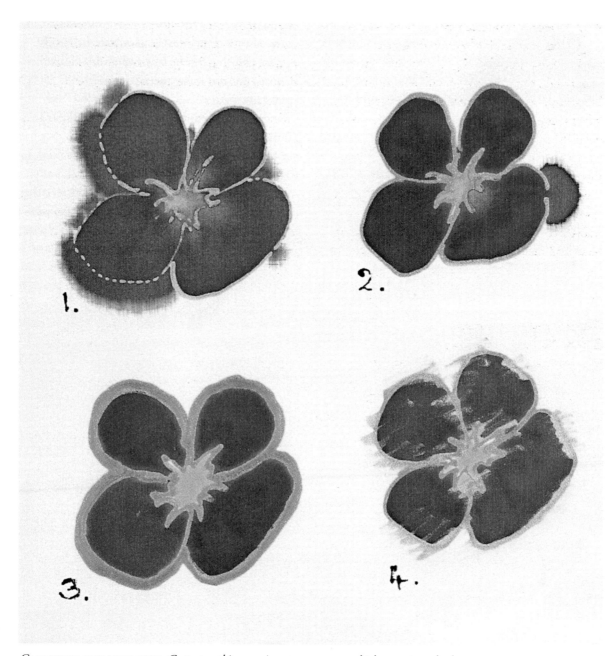

CLOCKWISE FROM TOP LEFT *Gutta too thin; gap in gutta; gutta too thick; gutta smudged*

of gutta. Adding too much dye will lessen the resist, so experiment and use your home-dyed guttas on practice samples first. If you require very deep colours you must use commercially coloured gutta, as the amount of dye you would need to add would weaken the resist too much for it to stop the paints from bleeding.

Avoid dry-cleaning articles that contain home-made gutta: they can bleed and run if they come into contact with certain dry-cleaning fluids.

METALLIC GUTTAS

Metallic guttas are simply guttas that have had a metallic colour added. They can be either water-based or spirit-based. They will remain on the surface of silk even after steaming. This will make your fabric slightly heavier than a clear gutta that washes away, leaving nothing on the fabric. It also means that metallic guttas aren't suitable for articles that require frequent washing as they will

shake it vigorously, and flush the water through, by squeezing the pipette hard, until the nib unblocks. This is also a good way to clean out your pipette. If you have used a spirit-based gutta, clean out the nib by pouring the gutta back into its original container and leaving the pipette turned upside down (in a disposable cup or something similar) until it has dried out. Dry gutta will form a thin film inside the pipette which is easy to remove with a cotton bud. Clean the nib in the same way.

WITHOUT AN APPLICATOR

Gutta can also be applied without an applicator. Try some of the following methods using gutta that has lumps or has, in any other way, passed its best. For all of the following techniques, except the last, the dyed silk can be fixed before you apply the gutta. This will make the silk a little stiffer, which is helpful if it is to be used for soft furnishings and cards. Stiffer silk is easier to cut and easier to mount into cards as lighter weight silk does not always lie flat. As it adds a little extra strength to the fabric, it can make sewing up soft furnishings easier.

Brushing

Use old artists' brushes for this technique as the gutta is quite difficult to remove. Pour the gutta onto a saucer; it is easier to dip your brush into this than into the gutta container. Using random strokes, paint the gutta onto the fabric. It will form a resisted area wherever it is placed, working in a similar to the wax in batik. Brush on metallic gutta to add definition to specific elements, such as flowers.

Sponging

Sponging is a lovely way to add texture to any piece of silk. Paint your silk in washes of orange and red for example. Pour your gutta into a pot or saucer and use either a household or natural sponge to apply it. Try cutting a household sponge into various shapes, or use foam stencilling blocks. Be careful not to overload the sponge with gutta: if you apply too much, you will lose the texture that a sponge gives.

Paper rolling

Dip rolled or crumpled paper into the gutta, being careful not to overload it, and wipe it over your silk. Try using various colours of gutta.

Splattering

If you feel like being adventurous and really enjoying yourself, try splattering. This is not the most accurate method of application, and not a good technique to try out in your kitchen – prop your frame up against a wall and cover the wall around it with paper or polythene. Use old brushes and toothbrushes to flick the gutta over the silk. Allow it to trickle down, turn the frame upside down so that it flows the other way, and when the splatters are dry, paint your silk. Experiment with different thicknesses of gutta.

DILUTING GUTTA

Try diluting your gutta with water if it is water-based, or Essence F if it is spirit-based. Lay your silk out flat or prop it up against something, then drop or dribble the gutta onto it from a spoon or a pipette with no nib. If the silk is flat, the drops will remain where they land, if it is propped up, the gutta will run in lines. Another effect can be achieved by trickling thinned gutta onto a silk background that has been sprayed with water or covered with dye. Or try this: paint a background in various colours and leave to dry. Water down some old, coloured, water-based gutta and, holding you frame upright, squeeze a stripe of the runny gutta across the the top. As it starts to run down, turn the frame and watch the direction of flow change. Squeeze more gutta across what is now the top of the frame, and continue in this way until you are satisfied with the result. For a stained-glass effect, wait until the dribbles are dry and then fill in the spaces between them with bright colours.

RIGHT *The effects produced by dribbling diluted gutta*

Project 1

RANDOM DESIGN CARDS

Getting used to gutta

1 Tear a piece of silk to fit your frame and pin it in place.

2 If you are working with clear gutta, try placing a sheet of coloured card underneath your silk. You'll be able to see what you're doing much more easily. However, remember to remove it before you start painting or it might alter your perception of the dye colours.

3 Draw a random pattern onto the silk. Try not to leave too many large areas; as they are usually harder to colour at this stage. Small areas tend to make more interesting cards. Allow to dry thoroughly.

4 Check for gaps in the gutta by holding the silk up to a light. If you find any holes, apply more gutta to seal them.

Random doodles with gutta

Doodles with deliberate gaps, allowing the dye to leak

5 Fill your palette with up to four colours and gradually paint in the areas of your design. It is very important to completely fill your brush with dye and then wipe off any excess into the palette. Under no circumstances should you allow the brush to drip. If you apply too much dye, it will jump over your gutta lines. If this does happen, use a hairdryer to stop the flow in the leaking area. Once it is dry, you can safely apply more gutta. Work from the centre of each area towards the gutta lines. This will avoid excessive watermarks forming. Do not paint right up to the gutta lines. If you add too much paint next to them, it might spill over the top. If you add dye to the centre each time, it will travel along the silk's fibres and stop at the gutta. Give the dye a chance to spread. If you think it isn't going to spread all the way to the lines, add a little more paint, this time slightly closer to the resist line. Be sure to do this before the original dye dries or you will create a watermark. The rate at which the dye dries will vary – it will dry more quickly if the room is warm and dry.

6 Once you have filled in the whole design, you can apply a metallic gutta over the top to add extra interest.

7 Follow the instructions for steam fixing on p 118 and mount into cards.

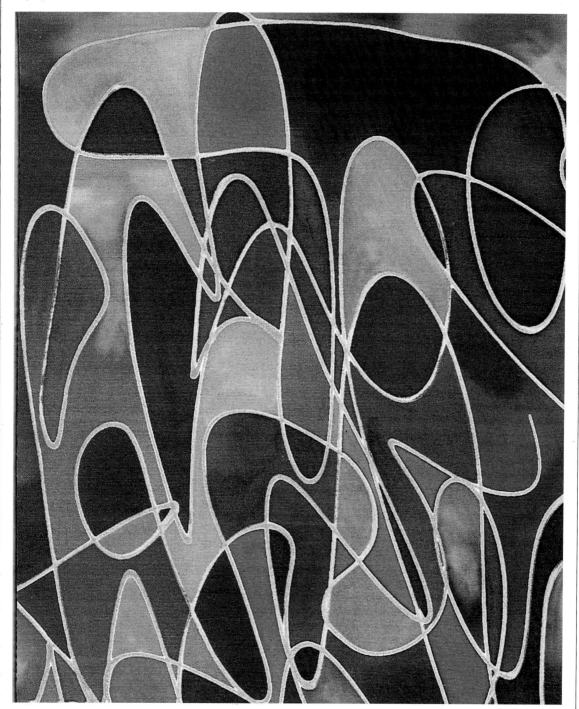

Filled doodles

Filled doodles with black gutta added after painting

PLANNING
YOUR WORK

Basic colour theory

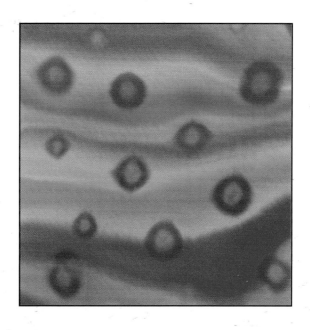

*Understanding the basic
language of colour will help
you visualize which colours
will go well together and
how to mix them.*

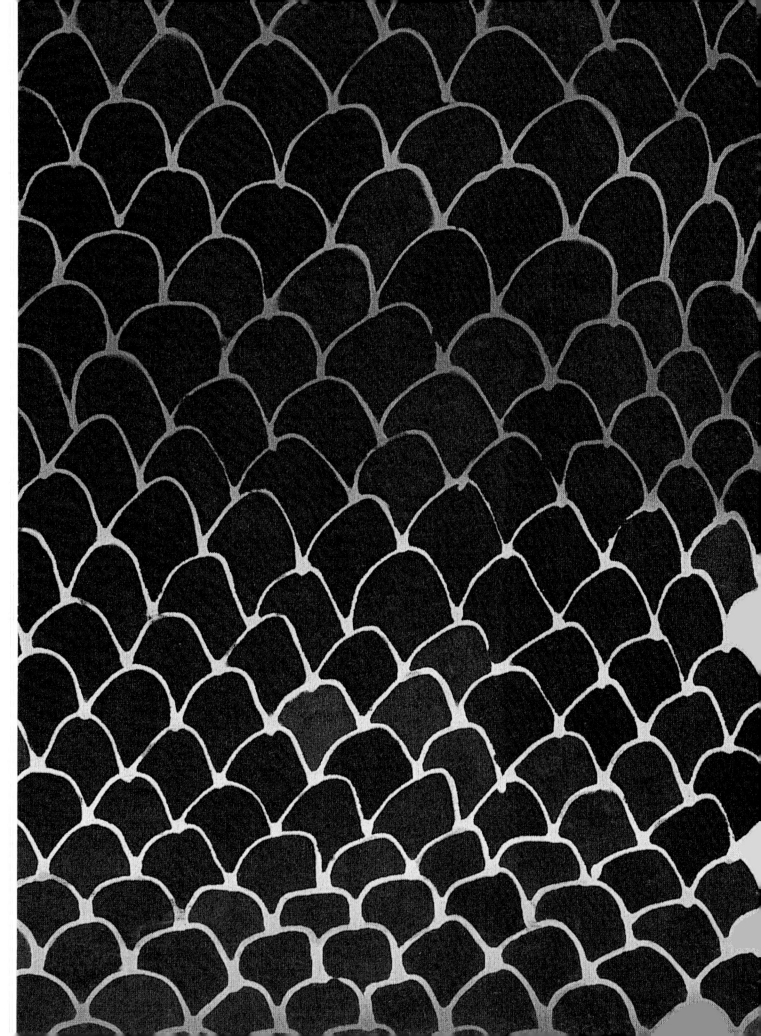

Choosing and transferring designs

When a scarf is draped around a neck, only a few sections remain visible, so it makes sense to place specific elements of the design in the places that will be seen. It is such a shame that some beautiful designs are lost when scarves are worn.

Gutta leaks before fixing

You don't need to be able to draw to enjoy silk painting. You can always trace images or doodle random designs, and you might find that you start to experiment. When you first start painting, your selection of designs is very important. They need to be stimulating enough to get you fired up and yet not so complicated that you will be disheartened if they don't work out as planned.

Books of stained-glass patterns are an excellent source of designs that are perfect for beginners, and give you the strong lines you need for gutta. Dover publishes such titles along subject themes, for example, sun catchers, birds and art nouveau. The beauty of these books is that they are all copyright-free and have spines that are made to lie completely flat when the book is opened up, making tracing much easier.

CHOOSING A DESIGN

Always try to choose a picture to which you can add elements, should you make a mistake. For example, if you are painting petals and your dye leaks through a hole in the gutta line, you can stop the flow with a hairdryer and then, when the dye is dry, outline extra leaves or petals in gutta, as in the example left. If you don't let anyone know there is a mistake, the chances are, no one will spot it.

It is very important that you dry your dye before adding more water-based gutta: if the dye is wet, the gutta and dye will blend together and the gutta will not hold.

TRANSFERRING DESIGNS

WATER-ERASABLE PENS
These pens are among the most useful items you can have, but make sure you buy the right type. Some are water and air erasable, others only air

Final version with repaired gutta and added petals

PREVIOUS PAGE *'Jug of flowers'*

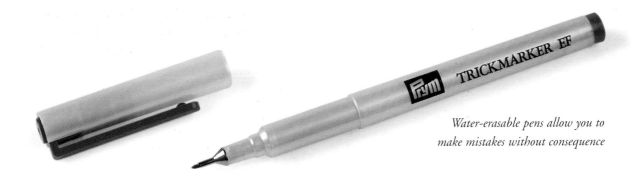

Water-erasable pens allow you to make mistakes without consequence

erasable and the marks from these can linger on and never really disappear. Check them out first; some shops will have a sample pen for you to test. With water-erasable pens you can draw on your silk, make any number of mistakes and not have to worry – your mistakes will disappear. When you paint over the pen marks with water, dye or gutta they will vanish; while some brands vanish straight away, others may take a few hours. Don't fall into the trap that I did! I drew a wonderful design, then left it to go and do something else. By the time I returned, my pen lines had gone.

THE REVERSING METHOD

The reverse method of transferring designs is great for those who enjoy painting but don't have enough confidence to create designs themselves. It's also good for tracing through thicker fabrics.

If your final design needs to face a certain direction, you can either reverse the design on a computer or use what is known as the eight pin method for reversing.

THE EIGHT-PIN METHOD

1 If necessary, enlarge your design.

2 Place this on your table and secure it with two small pieces of masking tape.

3 Pin the silk to your frame with eight pins, one at each corner and one in the middle of each side.

4 Turn your frame upside down so that the silk is lying flat against the table, over your design.

5 Trace your design with an erasable pen.

6 If your design needs reversing, unpin the silk, turn it upside down, then pin it to the frame again. The image will now be facing the right way. If it doesn't need reversing, simply turn your frame over and add the rest of the pins. Many people miss this step out and gutta their design to the table.

7 Apply your gutta now: if you leave it till later, your design will have disappeared.

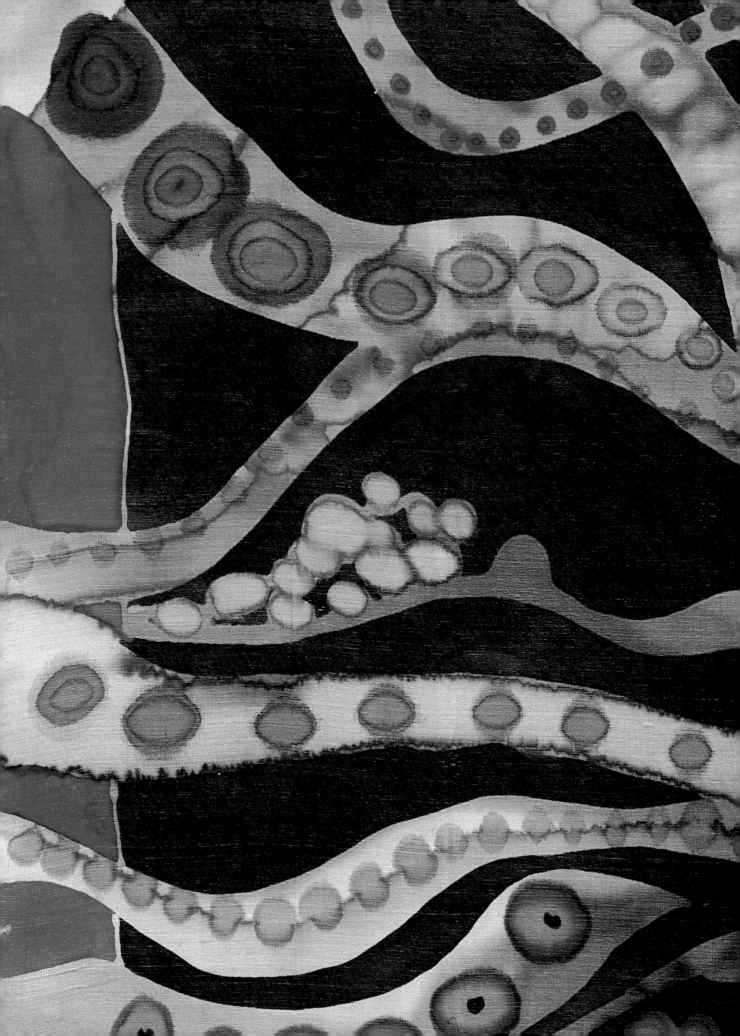

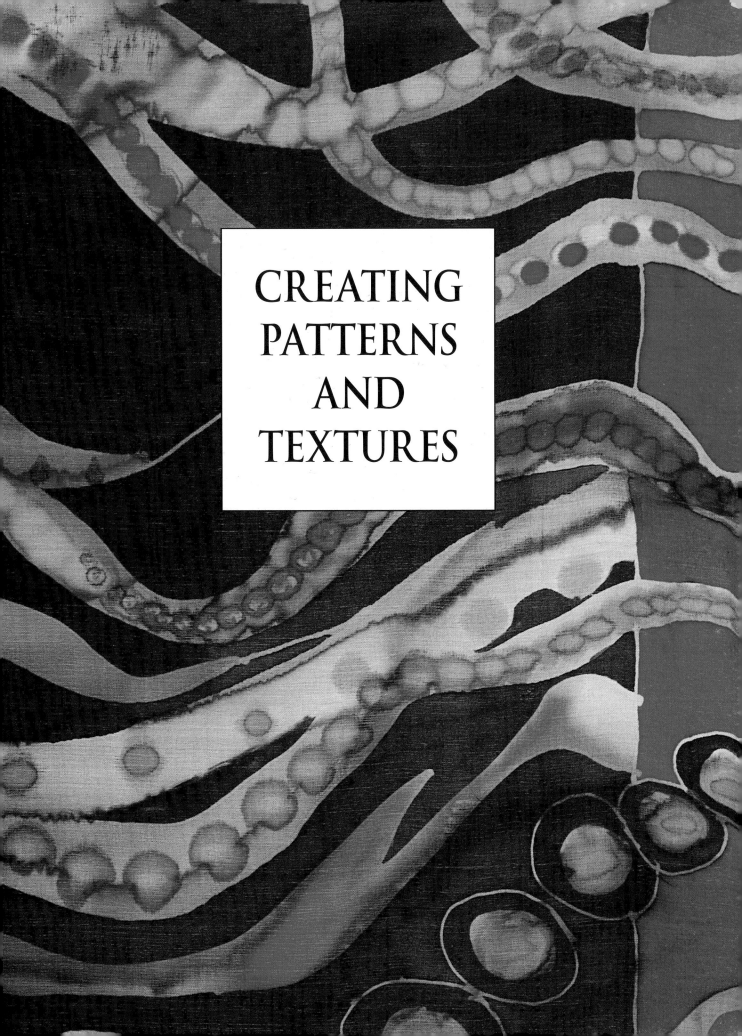

CREATING
PATTERNS
AND
TEXTURES

Salting and saline solutions

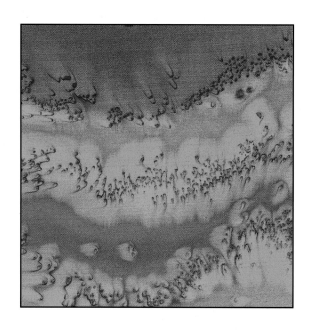

These techniques are simple and exciting. The salt changes the colours and designs on the silk, so the finished result is always an unexpected and pleasant surprise.

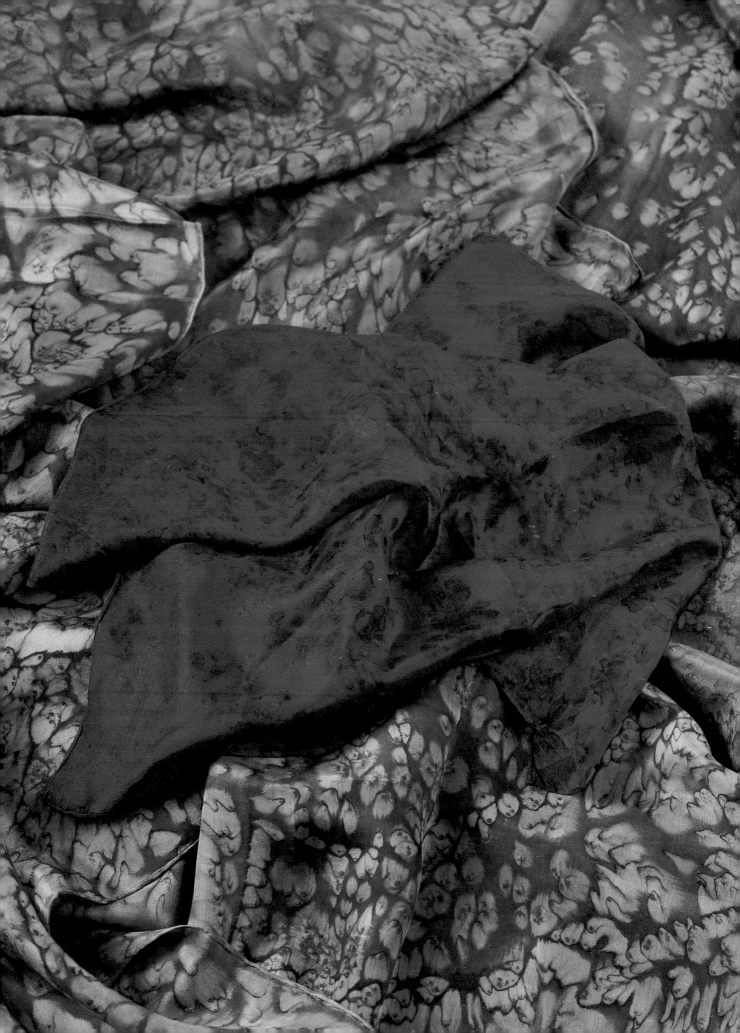

ost types of salt can be used – table salt, rock salt, even dishwasher salt – and each will react differently with the dyes. The smaller the grain of the salt, the finer the resultant detail. Table salt, for example, will give a fine, feathery effect while designs created with rock salt will be more bold. Rock salt is ideal for designs based on landscapes and trees. With dishwasher salt, I find the cheaper the better. The more expensive the salt, the smoother and more regular the grains tend to be, and such grains do not accept dyes as easily as irregular, rough grains. In some delicatessens you can buy salt in pearl grains and these give a lovely rounded finish.

PREVIOUS PAGE *Examples of the effects of salting*
BELOW *Here the salting has produced a feathery effect*

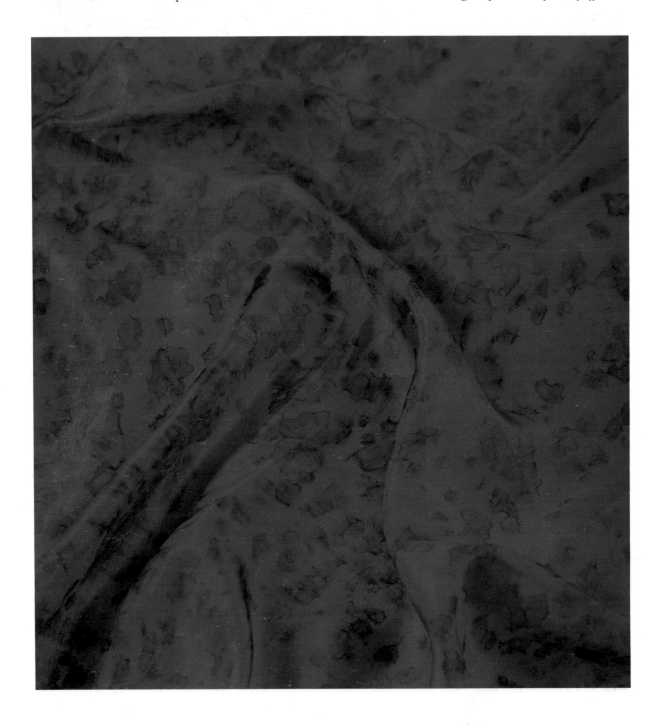

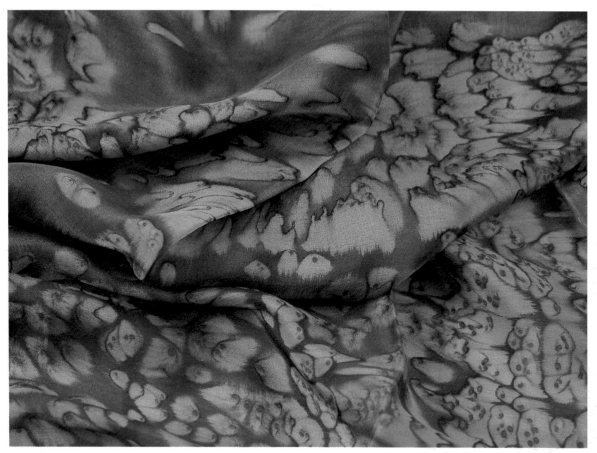

On this scarf the effect is more rounded

Special silk-painting salt will give a strong and fast result. Some manufacturers advise you to discard the salt after use but I have some that has been 'on the go' for years. Its effect isn't as strong as new salt, but for practising and for backgrounds it is fine. Just dry it out and keep it in a separate container from your unused salt.

If you want a strong effect use fresh salt, but if you are after something softer, use older salt. The one possible problem with old salt is that it might allow some dye to bleed back onto your work. Though this is unlikely, it is wise to try it on a test sample first.

The weight of the silk, the temperature of the salt, and the method of fixing will also affect the final result. The heavier the silk, the slower the dye will be drawn towards the salt; the warmer the salt, the faster it will draw in moisture.

Salting is one of the few techniques with which iron-fix dyes work better than steam-fix.

Make sure you don't get any salt in your dyes as you work: it will ruin them as it impedes their flowing action

APPLYING SALT

There are two main methods of applying salt: painting the silk first and then sprinkling it over the fabric while the dye is still wet, or placing the salt on the undyed silk and painting around it.

AFTER DYEING

Always sprinkle the salt evenly over your silk. Wherever you place a grain of salt, the water or dye will be drawn towards it, creating draglines and wonderful shapes. When the salt grains are full, the dye will pool underneath them and form a dark mark. You will need some practice to find the right amount of dye or water to use. If your

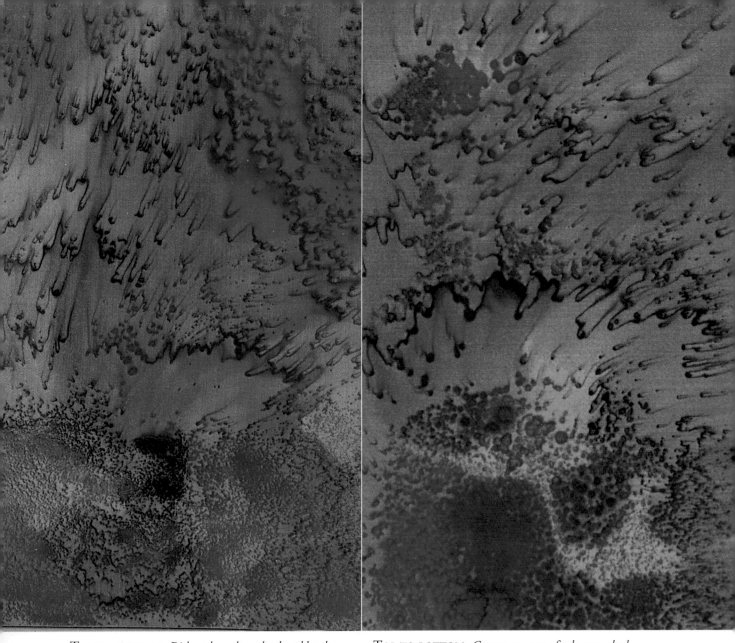

TOP TO BOTTOM *Dishwasher salt; rock salt; table salt*

TOP TO BOTTOM *Correct amount of salt; oversalted*

silk is too dry, you won't get any dragging and if your silk is too wet, the liquid might saturate the grains before they have a chance to work. If you use too many grains, the dye gets 'confused' and the result can be quite dark and hard to paint over. You may think that nothing is happening but wait a while and, before your eyes, the process will start. Try not to remove the salt until it has thoroughly dried.

BEFORE DYEING

This method is much more time-consuming, but it is effective. Use the tip of your brush to add dye around the salt grains. It is best not to remove the

salt until the dyes have completely dried. If you try to remove it while they are still wet or damp, you will smudge them. Do not use a hairdryer to hasten the process: you will blow salt all over the floor. Once the dye has dried, carefully brush the salt off. I use a small decorating brush for this.

You will probably find that some salt sticks, particularly if you are using gutta. If this is the case, use your fingernails to carefully prise it off. Because of salt's tendency to attract moisture, you must remove every grain before steaming. If you have to remove the salt before the dye has dried, turn your frame over and give it a few sharp taps.

Project 2

Observing the effects of salting

This experiment will work best with steam-fix dyes. Try it with both fresh and used salt.

1 Select a piece of silk and mark off four sections with gutta lines. Allow these to dry.

2 On the first section, paint a single coat of yellow.

3 Before the dye has dried, sprinkle on your salt. You will see that the salt pulls the dye towards it, but because there is not much pigment in yellow dye, the effect is a little dull. With this technique, dark colours work much better than light colours, such as yellow. However, black will not work. As the salt grains draw pigment towards them, a spot of concentrated pigment is left under each grain. To all intents and purposes, this looks black or near-black. It is these dark patches that create the texture with other colours, but with black, the patches are no darker than the original colour.

4 Once the dye has dried, remove the salt. It will remove most of the colour from a single, solid coat of dye, to lighten the whole wash.

5 Paint a single coat of a dark colour on the second section and sprinkle with salt. Once the salt has dried, remove it and compare the effect with the first section. This quarter should be nicely marked by the salt and have more texture.

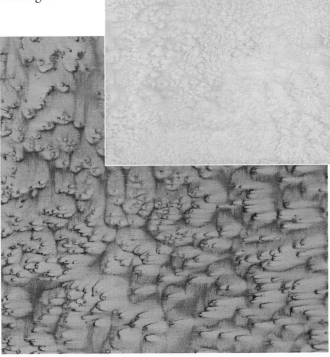

TOP *Salting on yellow dye*
RIGHT *Salting on blue dye*

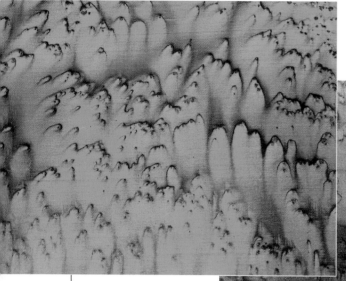

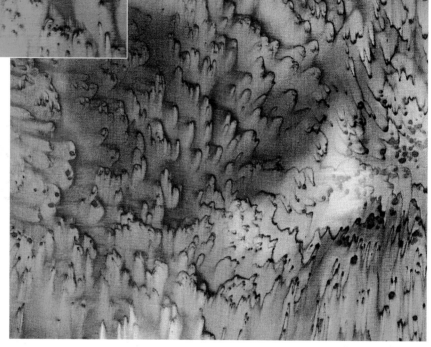

ABOVE *Salting on blue and green dye*
RIGHT *The effects of salting on a multi-coloured background*

6 On the third section, apply two or three colours randomly. Use a different brush for each, both to increase your speed of application and to prevent any muddying of colours.

7 Again, sprinkle on your salt while these dyes are still wet. You will see that as the salt draws in the dye, it mingles the colours.

8 For the final section, apply two or three colours randomly as for the third, but allow them to dry.

9 Make up a wash in a colour that will harmonize with the other three you have used. If you are using a fresh dye, mix half dye and half water, or make up a wash as described in the chapter on dyes (see p 30).

10 Using a large brush, paint this wash over the entire section. This will pull all of the colours together.

11 Sprinkle on the salt and watch the results.

Applying salt

For great results, try warming up the salt in the oven or on a radiator – warm salt pulls in moisture faster.

Salting can hide a multitude of sins. As a last resort, if you feel you can't save a piece of work, add more dye or water and sprinkle on some salt. Pieces salvaged in this way can make great cards.

A few deliberately placed grains of salt can produce fabulous effects (see the poppy head below). Try painting the centre of a sunflower brown, then paint on a few spots of yellow and carefully place a small amount of salt on each spot before the dye dries. Alternatively, paint some coloured stripes or circles and carefully place salt on the points where they meet.

While the poppy was still wet, I added a little dark purple to the centre and salted it to produce this effect

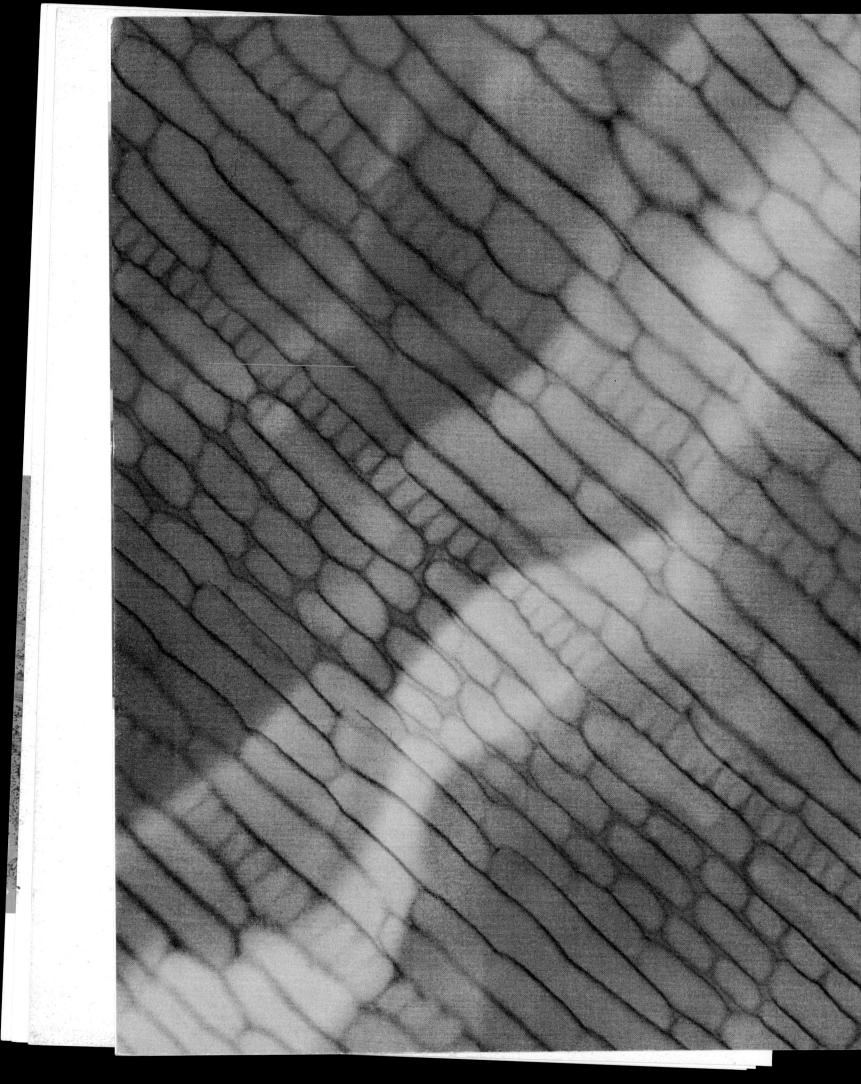

Surgical spirit is the safest form of alcohol to use and it is readily available from pharmacies. Other suitable spirits include methanol, medical alcohol, rubbing alcohol (70%), and methylated spirit. Bear in mind that such spirits are flammable, so store them carefully and, when you use them, always work in a well-ventilated room.

Different silks behave in different ways. Wild silk has such an uneven weave, it doesn't work well with alcohol, but crêpe de Chine works beautifully. Apply dye to several different types and weights of silk, let it dry, then spray or paint on alcohol (using brushes, cotton buds and swabs) and compare the effects.

To get the best results, your silk must be thoroughly dry. Fine details, such as veins on leaves and flowers, are easy to add if you use a fine brush. The alcohol dries almost immediately, so the dye doesn't get a chance to spread too far.

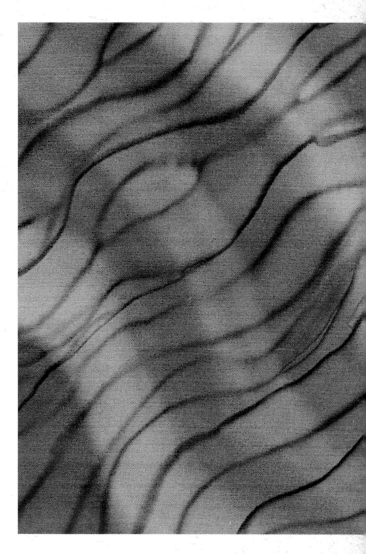

ABOVE *A wood-grain effect*
LEFT *This cell-like pattern was created by producing stripes and dots with alcohol*
ABOVE RIGHT *As the alcohol pushed the dye outwards, it created this texture of wavy stripes*

OMBRES

An ombré is a background of blended colours. The colours you use can have a dramatic effect on the feel of a picture. Try the technique below on a small piece of silk first.

STRIPES

1 Pour some yellow and some red into your palette and mix up a light and dark orange as well.

2 Paint your silk yellow.

3 While this yellow is still wet, paint on the light orange from the bottom to three-quarters of the way up the yellow.

Project 4

WATERMARKED SCARF

Dip-dyeing, spraying and creating watermarks

Watermarked scarves

1 Follow the dip-dyeing process for the salted scarf in Project 3 (see p 76) up to and including step 4, but using colours of your choice. (When making your selection, remember that darker colours will give you a better watermark, so they are the most suitable for this technique.)

2 Spray the silk randomly with your colours, then dry it thoroughly. Using a hairdryer for this will speed up the process dramatically, but try to keep your wet scarf from flapping, as any dye sitting in the hem can splash. Always keep your gloves on while you are drying painted silk or you will finish with dyed hands.

Watermarked oranges

3 Once the scarf is dry, lay it back on the table and carefully pin the corners to the polythene covering your work surface by inserting dressmakers' pins into the hem. This will keep it nice and flat.

4 Fill a pipette with clean water and use this to flick water onto the scarf. You will create a nicer mark flicking the pipette than squeezing it, as the dyes will not spread as quickly. For a different look, try applying the water in bands.

Pink-and-yellow tartan

THICKENER

Thickener, sometimes known as épaissisant, can also be used to create texture. Mix it with your dyes before painting the silk. It will appear quite shiny, but after fixing and washing this effect will be lost, leaving only stronger colour. Thickened dyes look much darker in the palette than on the silk; when you use them, remember that the finished results will always be a few shades lighter. They work well with sponging, blocking and mono printing, but it is best not to use a paint-brush to apply them to large areas as your brushstrokes will be clearly visible.

DILUENT

Diluents are ready-prepared chemicals that are used to dilute dyes. They separate the particles in a dye which promotes an even spread, helping to colour the silk with the minimum of streaks, watermarks and hard edges. A down side is that, if a diluent has been used, the effects of salting may not be as dramatic. Most are non-toxic, non-flammable and odourless, but always read the manufacturers' instructions before use, as brands do vary.

Generally, diluents will need diluting with water before use. An alternative to mixing them with the dye is to fill a spray bottle with the diluent in solution and spray this over the whole piece of silk before painting. This will keep the silk damp for longer than painting on a diluted dye, which will give you more time to work on your blending.

LEFT *Adding a diluent to a dye will produce a smooth, unbroken colour*
RIGHT *Without a diluent, the colours might be patchy and uneven*

Blending colours

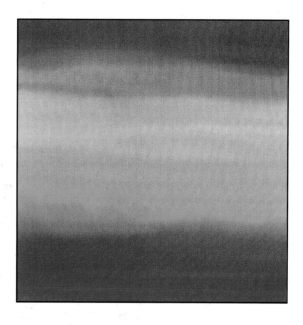

When you paint one colour next to another on dry silk, you might think that they would merge and blend. This could not be further from the truth; they will stop in an almost straight line.

2 Place a piece of paper over the fold
and rub it firmly with the back of a
spoon to make the fold crisp.

ABOVE *A design of pink magnolias with a background of
blended blues*
RIGHT *The same design and marbled background but
with the magnolias painted lemon*

MOUNTING SILK IN CARDS

A traditional way of mounting silk is flat-
mounting using a two- or three-fold card.
In the past I have been asked why it is necessary
to steam fix silk if it is going to be used to make
a card, which won't be washed. If you don't steam
silk and it gets wet or damp, the dyes will start
to move again and, in some circumstances, will
transfer to other surfaces. On top of this, you
won't get the beautiful sheen of the silk and the
intensity of colour that steaming brings.

3 Spray your piece of steamed and ironed silk
with two or three layers of hairspray or spray
starch. This will make it thicker, which makes
it easier to cut cleanly.

4 Iron the silk flat. It should now be as stiff
as paper and cut very easily. Cut out the shape
you require and, using an old brush, apply a
coating of PVA to the back; this will seal the
cut edges of the silk. Don't add too much or it
will seep through.

5 You are now free to decorate the silk as you desire. It will not fray for several weeks. If you use a thicker gutta line around your design and cut around it as close to the gutta as possible, this will prevent the silk from fraying, though enclosing it in a three-fold card would provide better protection for the finished piece than mounting it on the front of a two-fold card. If you have any rough or frayed edges showing, place glitter or ribbon around the edge of the silk.

THREE-FOLD CARDS

Three-fold cards come with a whole range of apertures including squares, ovals, christmas trees and even teddy bears. When mounting silk in three-fold cards, the most common mistakes are: cutting the silk the wrong size for the aperture and folding over the wrong piece of the card. If you follow the steps below, you will avoid both of these.

1 Trace the aperture onto a piece of paper and enlarge it by about 2in (5cm) all round.

2 Cut this template out and use it as a guide for cutting out your silk. Even though the edges will be covered by the card, you still need to ensure that it is cut neatly as the edges will show through when the light is behind the card.

3 With the inside of your card facing you, stick strips of double-sided tape around the aperture, making sure that none of them overlap it.

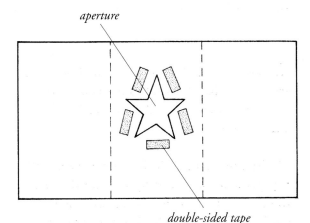

aperture

double-sided tape

Sticking tape around the aperture

4 Place your silk on the table, right side up. Take hold of your card and turn it over so that the sticky strips are facing downwards, but not touching the silk or the table. Move it around until the aperture is positioned correctly over your design. Once it is centred, drop the card down flat and rub it gently so that the tape picks up your silk.

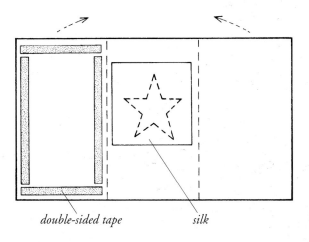

double-sided tape   *silk*

Positioning tape in preparation for covering the silk

5 Turn the card over and position further strips of tape on the left-hand side, as shown above.

6 Carefully fold the taped section over, making sure that it folds evenly, and smooth it down.

Overpainting

Overpainting is a technique that beats all others. At first it may appear that you are going nowhere fast but bear with it: you'll find the results amazing.

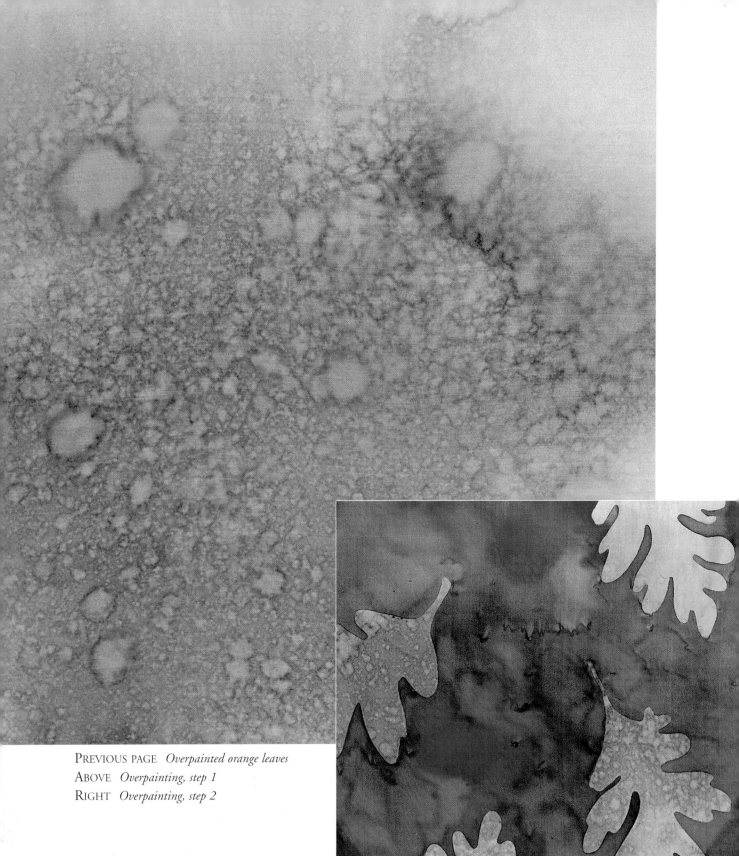

PREVIOUS PAGE *Overpainted orange leaves*
ABOVE *Overpainting, step 1*
RIGHT *Overpainting, step 2*

Overpainting, step 3

olourful autumn leaves are a very effective subject when treated in this way. I used an oak-leaf shape in these examples. With practice, this technique will become second nature, and you'll be able to use it without having to think too hard.

1 Paint your background in various colours (you can use spray bottles for this), making it as interesting as you can. Leave to dry.

2 Using clear gutta, draw on your leaf shapes. These outlines, and the patterns you draw inside the leaf shapes, won't be painted over again, so place them over the most attractive sections of the background. Allow the gutta to dry.

3 Using all the colours in your background except the lightest (save the lightest colour for the last layer of paint on the leaves to make them

stand out), paint over everything again, except the leaves. Introducing watermarks will add to the overall depth of the picture; some of the shading and patterns on the first layer will show through. Leave to dry.

4 Gutta on further leaves. Again, try to place these over the best parts of the background – places where colours meet etc.

5 When this gutta has dried paint the background once more, but don't paint inside any of your leaf shapes.

6 While this layer is still wet, add salt to selected areas. You now have the chance to repaint the initial leaves, depending on how you like the results. I always use yellow, adding it in the shape of veins, to create more watermarks. One example shown here has thin gold detail to finish it off.

ABOVE   *Overpainting, step 4*
RIGHT   *Close-up of overpainted leaves*
OPPOSITE   *The finished leaves*

OVERPAINTED SCALES

Another idea for overpainting is shown below.
Paint a striped pattern, using the ombré technique
(see p 85) to get nice blends of colour. Once this
has dried, add clear gutta in the shape of scales.
Leave this to dry, then paint in between the gutta
with the darkest colour you have. When this dries,
you'll see a myriad of colours shining through.

RIGHT *Step 1, ombréd background*
BELOW *The finished scales*

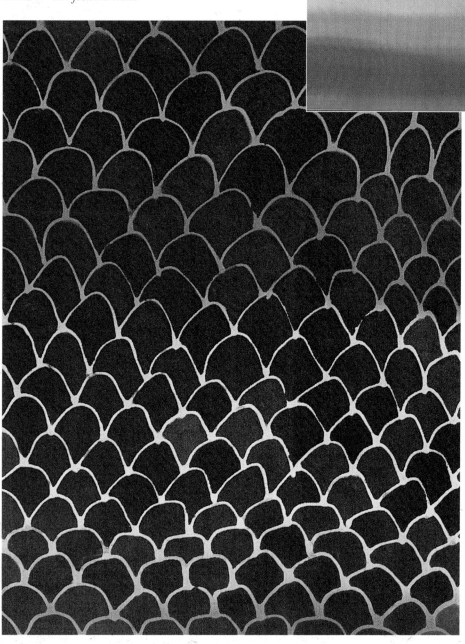

OPPOSITE *Two
designs created by
overpainting flowers*

Painting borders

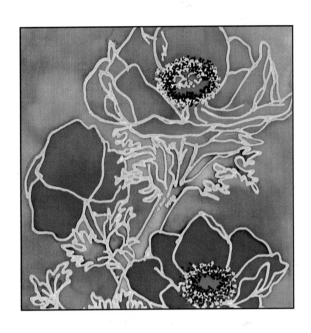

Painting a plain, unmarked border can be the most difficult technique to master. It must be done relatively fast to avoid watermarks forming. Until you gain confidence, it is best to design borders with breaks in them: this will allow you to paint each section more slowly, without worrying about marks.

This design has a split border

When you are painting a border, don't allow an area to dry before applying more dye to it, as this will cause watermarks to form. Never panic: if a border does not go according to plan, you can always save it by adding another pattern in gutta or by adding more dye and salting the whole thing.

A PERFECT BORDER

Follow the steps below for a perfect border. You'll see that you can easily get around large borders without watermarks.

1 Pin a medium-sized piece of silk onto a frame.

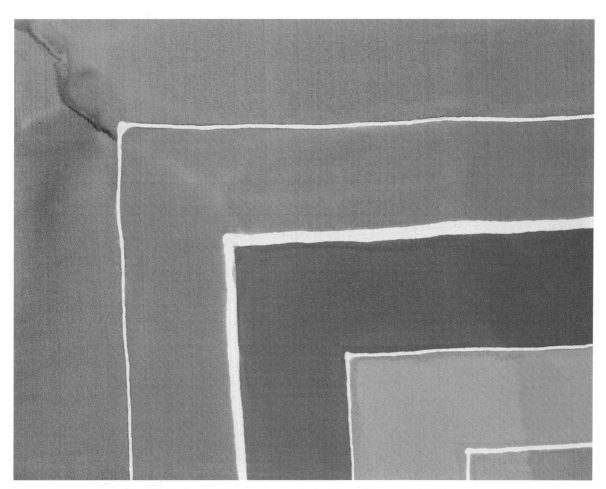

Green: this watermark is a typical mistake; Blue: correct method without diluent; Pink/gold: correct method with diluent

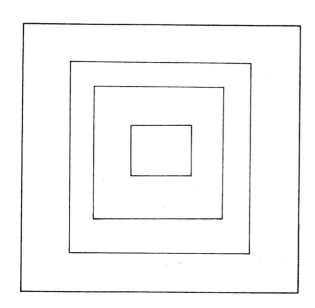

Practice squares for borders

2 Draw out a grid as shown left. Make sure you have a good amount of paint in your palette or jar and fill your brush or cotton wool with dye; you can hold more dye than you would for painting the main section of a scarf, but don't overfill. As you would with a brush, wipe the ball on the side of the pallette to prevent dripping.

3 Following the diagram on p 115, start at A and paint across to B.

4 Next, paint from A down to C and then, moving quickly, paint from B to D. Finally, paint from C to D. Keep an eye on where you've applied dye to ensure that it has spread all the way to the gutta line. As long as the dye is wet, you have plenty of time to go back and fill in any holes with a brush. Do not go back to any dry areas or your border will have watermarks.

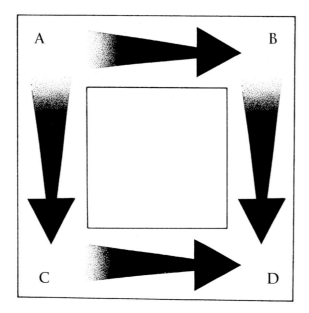

Method for painting borders

5 If you are adding a second layer of colour to your border, try to do so while the dye is still quite damp, and follow the same steps as for the first. If the first layer has dried, you should still follow the same steps, but you will probably need to work out any watermarks that form at the joins by rubbing the dye with your brush. Don't be afraid to press reasonably firmly – silk is very strong. You now have all the basic skills required to produce fabulous silk paintings; you just need the patience and time for practising.

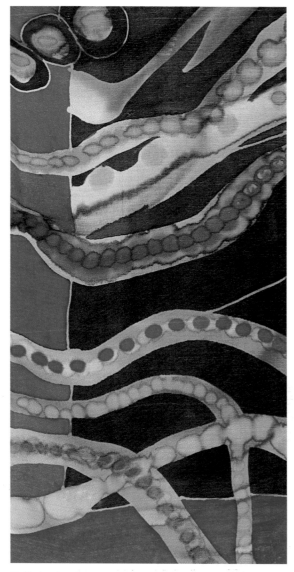

Split border close up

Palettes and brushes

◉ It is very important that you mix enough dye for your borders: there is little chance of you mixing more of the same colour in a hurry.

◉ The bigger the border you are painting, the bigger the brush you should use.

◉ If your palette is small, decant dye into a jar.

◉ You can use a ball of cotton wool, gripped with a peg, to give the same effect as a large brush. (Sponge brushes are great for applying water to large areas, but they soak up too much dye to use them for colour application.)

◉ Use decorating brushes to paint very large areas – they are cheap and very effective.

FIXING
YOUR
DYES

Steam fixing

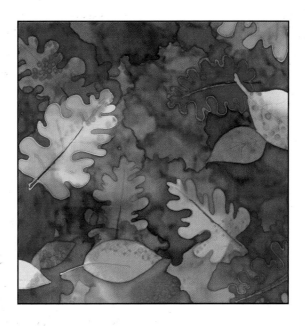

*Steam fixing can be daunting –
but only the first time you try.
Save all your practice scraps for
the following experiments
and you will soon feel
comfortable with the process.
The beauty of the colours and
the feel of the fabric after
steaming is amazing.*

'Dusk'

Steaming will add sheen to your silk and lustre to your colours but most importantly, it will prevent the colours running and bleeding should your silk get wet. Steam a few pieces at a time until you get the process right.

If you have a healthy bank account, you could buy yourself a basic professional steamer. These usually consist of a long, wide, metal tube with a lid and can accommodate up to 30m (33yds) of silk at a time. They need to be fixed to a water heating source, similar to a catering water boiler. The benefit of using professional steamers is that the silk does not get creased in any way, as it is rolled onto a thin tube like a broom handle. Alternatively, you could send your work off to

a professional to do the job for you. If you do this you must keep a note of which dyes, guttas and fabrics you have used so that the person steaming can get the timings right. For such a service you will be charged per metre (yard). Bear in mind that even a professional can't guarantee results.

DIY STEAMING

The cheapest, option is to steam the silk yourself. You will need some thin, absorbent paper such as wallpaper lining or plain newsprint paper – the type that takeaway food stores use is perfect. Ordinary printed newspaper can be used but it

GMC PUBLICATIONS

BOOKS

WOODTURNING

Adventures in Woodturning	*David Springett*
Bowl Turning Techniques Masterclass	*Tony Boase*
Chris Child's Projects for Woodturners	*Chris Child*
Colouring Techniques for Woodturners	*Jan Sanders*
Contemporary Turned Wood:	*Ray Leier, Jan Peters*
New Perspectives in a Rich Tradition	*& Kevin Wallace*
The Craftsman Woodturner	*Peter Child*
Decorating Turned Wood: The Maker's Eye	*Liz & Michael O'Donnell*
Decorative Techniques for Woodturners	*Hilary Bowen*
Illustrated Woodturning Techniques	*John Hunnex*
Intermediate Woodturning Projects	*GMC Publications*
Keith Rowley's Woodturning Projects	*Keith Rowley*
Making Screw Threads in Wood	*Fred Holder*
Turned Boxes: 50 Designs	*Chris Stott*
Turning Green Wood	*Michael O'Donnell*
Turning Pens and Pencils	*Kip Christensen & Rex Burningham*
Useful Woodturning Projects	*GMC Publications*
Woodturning: Bowls, Platters, Hollow Forms, Vases,	
Vessels, Bottles, Flasks, Tankards, Plates	*GMC Publications*
Woodturning: A Foundation Course (New Edition)	*Keith Rowley*
Woodturning: A Fresh Approach	*Robert Chapman*

UPHOLSTERY

The Upholsterer's Pocket Reference Book	*David James*
Upholstery: A Complete Course (Revised Edition)	*David James*
Upholstery Restoration	*David James*
Upholstery Techniques & Projects	*David James*
Upholstery Tips and Hints	*David James*

DOLLS' HOUSES AND MINIATURES

1/12 Scale Character Figures for the Dolls' House	*James Carrington*
Americana in 1/12 Scale: 50 Authentic Projects	*Joanne Ogreenc*
	& Mary Lou Santovec
Architecture for Dolls' Houses	*Joyce Percival*
The Authentic Georgian Dolls' House	*Brian Long*
A Beginners' Guide to the Dolls' House Hobby	*Jean Nisbett*
Celtic, Medieval and Tudor Wall Hangings	
in 1/12 Scale Needlepoint	*Sandra Whitehead*
Creating Decorative Fabrics: Projects in 1/12 Scale	*Janet Storey*
The Dolls' House 1/24 Scale: A Complete Introduction	*Jean Nisbett*
Dolls' House Accessories, Fixtures and Fittings	*Andrea Barham*
Dolls' House Furniture: Easy-to-Make Projects in 1/12 Scale	*Freida Gray*
Dolls' House Makeovers	*Jean Nisbett*
Dolls' House Window Treatments	*Eve Harwood*
Easy to Make Dolls' House Accessories	*Andrea Barham*
Edwardian-Style Hand-Knitted Fashion	
for 1/12 Scale Dolls	*Yvonne Wakefield*
How to Make Your Dolls' House Special:	
Fresh Ideas for Decorating	*Beryl Armstrong*
Make Your Own Dolls' House Furniture	*Maurice Harper*
Making Dolls' House Furniture	*Patricia King*
Making Georgian Dolls' Houses	*Derek Rowbottom*
Making Miniature Chinese Rugs and Carpets	*Carol Phillipson*
Making Miniature Food and Market Stalls	*Angie Scarr*
Making Miniature Gardens	*Freida Gray*
Making Miniature Oriental Rugs & Carpets	*Meik & Ian McNaughton*
Making Period Dolls' House Accessories	*Andrea Barham*
Making Tudor Dolls' Houses	*Derek Rowbottom*
Making Victorian Dolls' House Furniture	*Patricia King*
Miniature Bobbin Lace	*Roz Snowden*

Miniature Embroidery for the Georgian Dolls' House	*Pamela Warner*
Miniature Embroidery for the Tudor	
and Stuart Dolls' House	*Pamela Warner*
Miniature Embroidery for the Victorian Dolls' House	*Pamela Warner*
Miniature Needlepoint Carpets	*Janet Granger*
More Miniature Oriental Rugs & Carpets	*Meik & Ian McNaughton*
Needlepoint 1/12 Scale: Design Collections	
for the Dolls' House	*Felicity Price*
New Ideas for Miniature Bobbin Lace	*Roz Snowden*
The Secrets of the Dolls' House Makers	*Jean Nisbett*

CRAFTS

American Patchwork Designs in Needlepoint	*Melanie Tacon*
Beginning Picture Marquetry	*Lawrence Threadgold*
Blackwork: A New Approach	*Brenda Day*
Celtic Cross Stitch Designs	*Carol Phillipson*
Celtic Knotwork Designs	*Sheila Sturrock*
Celtic Knotwork Handbook	*Sheila Sturrock*
Celtic Spirals and Other Designs	*Sheila Sturrock*
Complete Pyrography	*Stephen Poole*
Creative Backstitch	*Helen Hall*
Creative Embroidery Techniques	*Daphne J. Ashby*
Using Colour Through Gold	*& Jackie Woolsey*
The Creative Quilter: Techniques and Projects	*Pauline Brown*
Cross-Stitch Designs from China	*Carol Phillipson*
Decoration on Fabric: A Sourcebook of Ideas	*Pauline Brown*
Decorative Beaded Purses	*Enid Taylor*
Designing and Making Cards	*Glennis Gilruth*
Glass Engraving Pattern Book	*John Everett*
Glass Painting	*Emma Sedman*
Handcrafted Rugs	*Sandra Hardy*
How to Arrange Flowers: A Japanese Approach	
to English Design	*Taeko Marvelly*
How to Make First-Class Cards	*Debbie Brown*
An Introduction to Crewel Embroidery	*Mave Glenny*
Making and Using Working Drawings	
for Realistic Model Animals	*Basil F. Fordham*
Making Character Bears	*Valerie Tyler*
Making Decorative Screens	*Amanda Howes*
Making Fabergé-Style Eggs	*Denise Hopper*
Making Fairies and Fantastical Creatures	*Julie Sharp*
Making Greetings Cards for Beginners	*Pat Sutherland*
Making Hand-Sewn Boxes: Techniques and Projects	*Jackie Woolsey*
Making Knitwear Fit	*Pat Ashforth & Steve Plummer*
Making Mini Cards, Gift Tags & Invitations	*Glennis Gilruth*
Making Soft-Bodied Dough Characters	*Patricia Hughes*
Natural Ideas for Christmas:	*Josie Cameron-Ashcroft*
Fantastic Decorations to Make	*& Carol Cox*
New Ideas for Crochet: Stylish Projects for the Home	*Darsha Capaldi*
Papercraft Projects for Special Occasions	*Sine Chesterman*
Patchwork for Beginners	*Pauline Brown*
Pyrography Designs	*Norma Gregory*
Pyrography Handbook (Practical Crafts)	*Stephen Poole*
Rose Windows for Quilters	*Angela Besley*
Rubber Stamping with Other Crafts	*Lynne Garner*
Sponge Painting	*Ann Rooney*
Stained Glass: Techniques and Projects	*Mary Shanahan*
Step-by-Step Pyrography Projects	
for the Solid Point Machine	*Norma Gregory*
Tassel Making for Beginners	*Enid Taylor*
Tatting Collage	*Lindsay Rogers*
Tatting Patterns	*Lyn Morton*

VIDEOS

MAGAZINES

WOODTURNING ◆ WOODCARVING ◆ FURNITURE & CABINETMAKING
THE ROUTER ◆ NEW WOODWORKING ◆ THE DOLLS' HOUSE MAGAZINE
OUTDOOR PHOTOGRAPHY ◆ BLACK & WHITE PHOTOGRAPHY
MACHINE KNITTING NEWS ◆ BUSINESSMATTERS

The above represents a full list of all titles currently published or scheduled to be published.
All are available direct from the Publishers or through bookshops, newsagents and specialist retailers.
To place an order, or to obtain a complete catalogue, contact:

GMC PUBLICATIONS

Castle Place, 166 High Street, Lewes, East Sussex BN7 1XU, United Kingdom
Tel: 01273 488005 Fax: 01273 478606
E-mail: pubs@thegmcgroup.com

Orders by credit card are accepted